CONTENTS

INTRODUCTION

The New Testament contains numerous parables attributed to Jesus, but the exact number of parables varies depending on the criteria used for defining what constitutes a "parable," as well as the version of the Bible one consults. Many of these parables appear in the Synoptic Gospels: Matthew, Mark, and Luke. The Gospel of John contains fewer parables, and they are typically more allegorical in nature. Some are shorter and more akin to proverbial sayings, while others are more elaborate. But, for the sake of 'getting them all,' I also included those passages.

In the Gospel of Matthew:

    1. The Sower

    2. The Weeds Among the Wheat

    3. The Mustard Seed

    4. The Leaven

    5. Hidden Treasure

    6. The Pearl of Great Price

    7. The Dragnet

    8. The Unforgiving Servant

9. The Laborers in the Vineyard

10. The Two Sons

11. The Wicked Tenants

12. The Great Banquet

13. The Wedding Feast

14. The Ten Virgins

15. The Talents

16. The Sheep and the Goats (sometimes considered a parable)

17. New Cloth on an Old Garment and New Wine in Old Wineskins

18. The Lost Sheep (a different version from Luke's)

In the Gospel of Mark:

1. The Sower

2. The Seed Growing Secretly

3. The Mustard Seed

4. New Cloth on an Old Garment and New Wine in Old Wineskins

In the Gospel of Luke:

1. The Sower

2. The Lamp Under a Jar

3. The Wise and the Foolish Builders

4. The Mustard Seed

5. The Leaven

6. The Good Samaritan

7. The Friend at Midnight

8. The Rich Fool

9. The Barren Fig Tree

10. The Great Banquet

11. The Lost Sheep

12. The Lost Coin

13. The Prodigal Son

14. The Dishonest Manager

15. The Rich Man and Lazarus

16. The Unjust Judge

17. The Pharisee and the Tax Collector

18. The Ten Minas

19. New Cloth on an Old Garment and New Wine in Old Wineskins

In the Gospel of John:

1. The Good Shepherd (often considered an allegory)

2. The Vine and the Branches (often considered an allegory)

When you account for additional parables or parabolic sayings that are sometimes included, the count can exceed 40. Depending on one's interpretative approach to the texts, this expanded list may still not be exhaustive. Some scholars also consider parallels or alternative versions of the same basic story (like the Lost Sheep in Matthew and Luke) separate entries, while others do not.

General Themes in Matthew's Parables

Let's discuss the overarching themes found in the parables unique to or prominently featured in the Gospel of Matthew. These themes can help readers understand the primary messages Matthew aimed to convey through Jesus' teachings:

Kingdom of Heaven

Many of Matthew's parables, such as the Parable of the Sower, the Mustard Seed, and the Net, focus on the Kingdom of Heaven, describing its various dimensions—its growth, inclusivity, and the varied responses it elicits from people.

Judgment and Accountability

Parables like the Wheat and the Weeds, the Talents, and the Sheep and the Goats focus on the theme of final judgment. These stories emphasize personal responsibility and the moral and spiritual accountability that will come at the end times.

Repentance and Grace

The Parable of the Lost Sheep in Matthew echoes the theme of God's grace and the joy that comes from repentance and return to the fold, reinforcing the idea that God is not willing for any to perish but for all to come to repentance.

Hidden Treasure

The theme of the inestimable value of the Kingdom of Heaven is highlighted in parables like the Hidden Treasure and the Pearl of Great Price, where the protagonists go to great lengths to secure treasures that symbolize the kingdom.

Ethical Living and Moral Integrity

Parables such as the Unforgiving Servant focus on the ethical dimensions of life, including the importance of forgiveness, mercy, and other moral virtues as they relate to life within the Kingdom of Heaven.

Paradox and Reversal

Some parables in Matthew present a form of paradox or reversal of expectations. The Workers in the Vineyard highlights God's grace that often defies human notions of fairness. Similarly, the Parable of the Two Sons challenges preconceived notions of obedience and rebellion.

Immediate Action and Preparedness

Matthew's parables also express the urgency of response to the message of Jesus. Parables like the Wise and Foolish Virgins emphasize preparedness for the unexpected coming of the Kingdom.

Obedience to God's Will

The Parable of the Two Sons and the Parable of the Tenants put forth the idea that saying yes to God is not enough; actions must align with words, emphasizing the necessity of genuine obedience to God's will.

Human Relationships and Community

Parables like the Unforgiving Servant and the Sheep and the Goats extend the conversation into ethical living in community, discussing themes such as forgiveness, mercy, and altruism in a social context.

Each of these themes contributes to Matthew's broader theological and ethical points, creating a rich and multifaceted portrayal of the teachings of Jesus.

The Gospel of Matthew contains a wealth of parables, many of which are organized into discourses. Here's a brief point-form summary for each:

The Sower (Matthew 13:3-9, 18-23)

- **Summary**: Sower scatters seed on different types of soil with varying results.

- **Key Themes**: The various ways people respond to the word of God.

The Tares (Matthew 13:24-30, 36-43)

- **Summary**: Wheat and weeds grow together until the harvest.

- **Key Themes**: The coexistence of good and evil; final judgment.

The Mustard Seed (Matthew 13:31-32)

- **Summary**: Tiny mustard seed grows into a large tree.

- **Key Themes**: Growth and expansion of the Kingdom of God.

The Leaven (Matthew 13:33)

- **Summary**: Leaven permeates a large amount of dough.

- **Key Themes**: Pervasive influence of the Kingdom of God.

The Hidden Treasure (Matthew 13:44)

- **Summary**: Man finds treasure in a field and buys the field.

- **Key Themes**: The inestimable value of the Kingdom of God.

The Pearl of Great Price (Matthew 13:45-46)

- **Summary**: Merchant sells everything to buy a valuable pearl.

- **Key Themes**: Sacrifice for the incomparable worth of the Kingdom.

The Dragnet (Matthew 13:47-50)

- **Summary**: Net gathers fish of all kinds, sorted later.

- **Key Themes**: Inclusivity and final judgment in the Kingdom of God.

The Unforgiving Servant (Matthew 18:23-35)

- **Summary**: Servant forgiven huge debt but doesn't forgive a smaller one.

- **Key Themes**: Forgiveness and divine justice.

The Workers in the Vineyard (Matthew 20:1-16)

- **Summary**: Laborers hired at different times receive the same pay.

- **Key Themes**: God's generosity; equality in the Kingdom.

The Two Sons (Matthew 21:28-32)

- **Summary**: One son refuses to work but does, the other agrees but doesn't.

- **Key Themes**: Actions over words; repentance.

The Tenants (Matthew 21:33-46)

- **Summary**: Tenants kill the son of the vineyard owner.

- **Key Themes**: Israel's leaders' unfaithfulness; Jesus as the cornerstone.

The Wedding Banquet (Matthew 22:1-14)

- **Summary**: Invited guests refuse to come, others are brought in.

- **Key Themes**: Rejection and acceptance of God's invitation.

The Ten Virgins (Matthew 25:1-13)

- **Summary**: Five wise and five foolish virgins await a bridegroom.

- **Key Themes**: Preparedness for the return of Christ.

The Talents (Matthew 25:14-30)

- **Summary**: Servants given talents; rewarded or punished based on usage.

- **Key Themes**: Stewardship and accountability.

The Sheep and the Goats (Matthew 25:31-46)

- **Summary**: Final judgment based on acts of compassion.

- **Key Themes**: Ethical living; eschatological judgment.

New Cloth on an Old Garment & New Wine in Old Wineskins (Matthew 9:16-17)

- **Summary**: New cloth and new wine are incompatible with old garments and old wineskins.

- **Key Themes**: The newness of Jesus' teachings; incompatibility with old religious forms.

THE SOWER (MATTHEW 13:3-9, 18-23)

Context

The parable of the Sower is one of the most famous parables and is found in all three Synoptic Gospels (Matthew, Mark, and Luke). It is part of a series of parables in Matthew 13 that describe various aspects of the Kingdom of Heaven. This particular parable serves as an introduction to others and even includes an explanation given by Jesus to his disciples.

Summary

In the parable, a sower scatters seeds on four types of soil:

1. **The Path:** Birds come and eat up the seeds.

2. **Rocky Ground:** Seeds spring up quickly but wither because they have no depth of soil.

3. **Thorns:** Seeds grow but are choked by the thorns.

4. **Good Soil:** Seeds grow and produce a good crop, some hundred-fold, some sixty, some thirty.

Interpretation

Jesus himself interprets this parable for his disciples. Each type of soil represents a different response to God's word:

1. **The Path:** Those who hear the word of the kingdom and do not understand it; the evil one snatches what has been sown.

2. **Rocky Ground:** Those who hear the word and receive it with joy but have no root, enduring only for a while.

3. **Thorns:** Those who hear the word but are choked by the cares of the world and the lure of wealth.

4. **Good Soil:** Those who hear the word, understand it, and bear fruit.

Theological Implications

This parable is often interpreted as a commentary on the diverse responses to the message of the Kingdom of God. It emphasizes the role of human agency and freedom in receiving or rejecting God's word. The "fruit" doesn't only signify numerical or material abundance but also spiritual and moral qualities like faith, hope, and love.

Points for Reflection

- It's worth considering what kind of "soil" we are and how open or receptive we are to spiritual truths.

- This parable raises questions about evangelism and the role of the "sower." Who is the sower today, and how should the sowing be done?

The Weeds Among the Wheat (Matthew 13:24-30, 36-43)

Context

This parable is also part of the series in Matthew 13 that describes various aspects of the Kingdom of Heaven. It comes right after the Parable of the Sower and is closely related to it in terms of theme, but it explores a slightly different facet of the kingdom. Like the Sower, this parable also includes an explicit explanation given by Jesus to his disciples.

Summary

A man sows good seed in his field, but while everyone sleeps, his enemy sows weeds among the wheat. When the plants come up and bear grain, the weeds appear as well. The owner instructs his servants to let both grow together until the harvest. At this point, the weeds will be collected and burned, while the wheat will be gathered in the barn.

Interpretation

Jesus explains that the field is the world, and the good seed represents the "children of the kingdom." The weeds are the "children of the evil one," and the enemy who sows them is the devil. The harvest is the end of the age, and the reapers are angels. Just as the weeds are collected and burned, so will it be at the end of the age—there will be a separation of the evil from the righteous.

Theological Implications

This parable deals with the problem of evil and the eschatological (end-time) judgment. It teaches that both good and evil will coexist in the world until a final reckoning. Importantly, it advises against trying to uproot the evil prematurely, which could also harm the good.

Points for Reflection

- The parable has been interpreted as a caution against a rush to judgment and a call for patience and discernment.

- It may challenge us to consider how we interact with the "weeds" in our communities. Do we rush to judgment, or do we allow for the possibility of transformation and growth?

The Mustard Seed (Matthew 13:31-32)

Context

This is another parable from Matthew 13, immediately following the Parable of the Weeds Among the Wheat. It's one of the shorter parables and is also found in Mark and Luke.

Summary

A man takes a mustard seed and plants it in his field. Even though the mustard seed is one of the smallest of all seeds, it grows into a tree where birds come to nest.

Interpretation

The mustard seed represents the Kingdom of Heaven, which starts from small beginnings but grows into something large and influential. The birds nesting in its branches may signify that the kingdom provides shelter and sustenance.

Theological Implications

The parable is often seen as a message of hope and encouragement, emphasizing the transformative power of small acts of faith or goodness. It also serves as a metaphor for how the message of Jesus would start with a small group but eventually spread to many nations.

Points for Reflection

- This parable encourages us not to despise small beginnings. Even small acts in line with the kingdom's values can have a significant impact.

- It also might make us ponder on what "seeds" we are planting in our lives and what kind of "tree" they are growing into.

THE LEAVEN (MATTHEW 13:33)

Context

Like the Parable of the Mustard Seed, the Parable of the Leaven is part of the string of parables in Matthew 13 and is also relatively brief. It focuses on the transformative nature of the Kingdom of Heaven.

Summary

A woman mixes a small amount of leaven (yeast) into a large quantity of flour until the whole batch is leavened.

Interpretation

The yeast works quietly and pervasively to influence a much larger body of dough. Similar to the mustard seed, this parable describes how something small and seemingly insignificant can have a huge impact. The yeast represents the Kingdom of Heaven, and its mixing with the dough signifies the transformative effect of God's reign.

Theological Implications

This parable emphasizes the permeating and transformative power of the Kingdom. It shows that even a small amount of influence or a simple act can have large-scale effects when aligned with the principles of God's Kingdom.

Points for Reflection

- The parable prompts us to consider our "leavening" influence in our respective spheres. How do we contribute to the transformation of society in alignment with Kingdom values?

- Like yeast, the Kingdom of Heaven works subtly but effectively, asking us to reconsider the ways we look for evidence of God's work in the world.

Hidden Treasure (Matthew 13:44)

Context

The parable of the Hidden Treasure, like the Parables of the Mustard Seed and the Leaven, is short and found in Matthew 13. It deals with the incomparable value of the Kingdom of Heaven.

Summary

A man finds a treasure hidden in a field. Filled with joy, he hides it again and sells all he has to buy the field.

Interpretation

The man's joyful sacrifice to obtain the field represents the radical decision to follow Christ and enter the Kingdom of Heaven. The treasure symbolizes the immense value and joy of the Kingdom, which surpasses all earthly possessions and ambitions.

Theological Implications

This parable portrays the Kingdom of Heaven as something so valuable that it is worth giving up everything to gain it. It emphasizes the joy that accompanies this discovery and sacrifice.

Points for Reflection

- The parable prompts us to think about what we consider "treasure" and how those considerations align with Kingdom values.

- It also invites us to reflect on the sacrifices we are willing to make for what we consider to be of ultimate importance.

The Pearl of Great Price (Matthew 13:45-46)

Context

This parable is in close thematic alignment with the Parable of the Hidden Treasure and follows it in Matthew 13. It also addresses the immeasurable value of the Kingdom of Heaven.

Summary

A merchant in search of fine pearls finds one of great value. He goes away and sells everything he has to buy it.

Interpretation

Similar to the Hidden Treasure, this parable emphasizes the inestimable worth of the Kingdom of Heaven. The merchant is actively seeking fine pearls, indicating a conscious spiritual quest. When he finds the pearl of great value, he willingly sacrifices all he has for it.

Theological Implications

The parable highlights the preciousness of the Kingdom and suggests that it is worth every sacrifice. It also speaks to those who are actively seeking spiritual truth, suggesting that the ultimate "pearl" is the Kingdom of Heaven.

Points for Reflection

- This parable challenges us to assess what we are actively seeking in our lives and what we are willing to sacrifice to find it.

- It also invites us to consider whether our quest for spiritual or moral excellence has led us to discover something of incomparable worth.

THE NET (MATTHEW 13:47-50)

Context

This parable concludes the series in Matthew 13 and mirrors some of the themes found in the Parable of the Weeds Among the Wheat, especially the eschatological sorting of good and bad.

Summary

A net is thrown into the sea and gathers fish of every kind. When it is full, it is pulled ashore, and the good fish are sorted into containers while the bad ones are thrown away.

Interpretation

Jesus interprets this parable as another allegory of the end times. The net symbolizes the close of the age, where the angels will separate the evil from the righteous, much like the sorting of the fish.

Theological Implications

This parable reiterates the themes of divine judgment and the coexistence of good and evil until the end of the age. It serves as a reminder of the ultimate accountability that awaits everyone.

Points for Reflection

- The parable invites us to consider our own readiness for the "sorting" at the end of the age. How does this impending reality affect our daily choices and actions?

- It also prompts reflection on the idea of judgment itself. What does it mean for God to separate the "good" from the "bad," and how does this square with notions of divine love and justice?

THE UNFORGIVING SERVANT (MATTHEW 18:21-35)

Context

This parable is situated in a section of Matthew that deals with relationships within the Christian community, especially the need for forgiveness and reconciliation. Peter asks Jesus how often he should forgive a brother who sins against him, and Jesus replies with this parable.

Summary

A king decides to settle accounts with his servants. One servant owes him an enormous sum that he cannot pay. The king orders that the servant and his family be sold to repay the debt. The servant begs for mercy, and the king forgives him. However, this servant goes out and harshly demands repayment from another servant who owes him a much smaller amount. When the king hears about this, he reinstates the first servant's debt and throws him into prison.

Interpretation

The king represents God, and the servants symbolize human beings. The enormous debt of the first servant is a metaphor for the sins that humanity owes to God. The parable illustrates the importance of showing mercy and forgiveness to others, especially when we ourselves have received it.

Theological Implications

This parable highlights the principle of reciprocal mercy and forgiveness. It reflects the petition in the Lord's Prayer: "Forgive us our debts, as we also have forgiven our debtors." It emphasizes that our forgiveness from God is intertwined with our ability to forgive others.

Points for Reflection

- This parable forces us to examine our own attitudes toward forgiveness. Are we willing to extend the grace we have received to others?

- It also raises questions about the nature of God's forgiveness. Is divine forgiveness conditional upon our actions, or is it an unconditional gift?

THE LABORERS IN THE VINEYARD (MATTHEW 20:1-16)

Context

This parable is found in a section that discusses the values of the Kingdom of Heaven, particularly issues of fairness and reward. It directly follows a conversation where Peter asks what the disciples will get for having left everything to follow Jesus.

Summary

A landowner hires laborers at different times throughout the day but pays them all the same wage—a denarius—at the end. Those who worked the longest hours complain, but the landowner insists that he has not cheated anyone and that he has the right to be generous.

Interpretation

The landowner symbolizes God, and the workers represent various people who enter the Kingdom at different "times" in their lives. The parable challenges conventional notions of fairness by introducing God's radical generosity and grace.

Theological Implications

This parable focuses on the theme of divine generosity that transcends human ideas of fairness. It suggests that the last will be first and the first last, challenging the human tendency to compare and measure worth by effort or merit.

Points for Reflection

- This parable challenges us to consider our own views on fairness and reward, particularly in spiritual matters. Do we begrudge God's generosity to others?

- It also raises questions about entitlement and grace. Do we feel entitled to God's blessings or see them as a gift?

The Two Sons (Matthew 21:28-32)

Context

This parable comes in a section where Jesus is teaching in the temple and is confronted by the chief priests and elders. It serves as a response to their challenge to his authority.

Summary

A man asks his two sons to go work in the vineyard. The first son initially refuses but later changes his mind and goes. The second son agrees to go but doesn't follow through. Jesus asks which of the two did the will of the father, to which the answer is the first son.

Interpretation

The two sons represent different responses to God's call to righteousness. The first son's change of heart and eventual obedience is likened to tax collectors and sinners who repent and enter the Kingdom of Heaven. The second son's empty promise represents the religious leaders who claim righteousness but do not genuinely obey God.

Theological Implications

This parable emphasizes the importance of repentance and sincere obedience over mere verbal assent. It challenges religious complacency and underscores the idea that actions speak louder than words.

Points for Reflection

- The parable prompts us to consider the sincerity of our own commitments. Are we more like the first son or the second son in our spiritual journey?

- It also challenges us to think about the dynamics of repentance and transformation. How open are we to changing our path when confronted with the need to do so?

THE WICKED TENANTS (MATTHEW 21:33-46)

Context

This parable also comes in the context of Jesus' confrontations with the religious leaders in Jerusalem just after the Parable of the Two Sons. It serves as a strong critique of the religious leadership and a prophetic statement about the coming rejection of Jesus.

Summary

A landowner plants a vineyard and rents it to tenants. When he sends servants and later his son to collect the produce, the tenants beat the servants and kill the son. The landowner eventually comes to destroy the wicked tenants and give the vineyard to others.

Interpretation

The landowner represents God, the vineyard is Israel, the tenants are the religious leaders, the servants are the prophets, and the son is Jesus. The parable predicts the rejection and crucifixion of Jesus and suggests that the religious leadership will lose their authority.

Theological Implications

This parable introduces themes of judgment and the shifting of religious authority due to unfaithfulness. It also serves as a prophetic allegory concerning the life and mission of Jesus.

Points for Reflection

- The parable is a critique of religious leadership but can also be a warning for anyone entrusted with responsibilities from God. Are we faithful stewards?

- It makes us ponder on the gravity of rejecting God's messengers and His Son, prompting reflection on how open we are to divine guidance and correction.

The Wedding Feast (Matthew 22:1-14)

Context

This parable is spoken to the chief priests and Pharisees and comes after a series of confrontations between Jesus and the religious authorities. Like some other parables, it is an allegory that depicts God's relationship with Israel and the coming of the Kingdom.

Summary

A king sends out invitations for his son's wedding feast, but the invited guests refuse to come. Some even mistreat and kill the king's servants. The king then invites everyone, good and bad, to fill the wedding hall. However, one man without a wedding garment is thrown out.

Interpretation

The king represents God, and the son symbolizes Jesus. The first invited guests are the people of Israel, and their refusal signifies Israel's general rejection of Jesus. The second group of invitees represents the inclusion of Gentiles in the Kingdom. The man without a wedding garment symbolizes those who try to enter without true righteousness.

Theological Implications

The parable presents themes of invitation, rejection, and judgment. It depicts God's generous invitation to the Kingdom, the tragic refusal by many, and the opening of the Kingdom to all, albeit with conditions.

Points for Reflection

- This parable calls us to reflect on how we respond to God's invitations in our lives. Do we accept with eagerness, or do we make excuses?

- The fate of the man without a wedding garment warns against complacency; being "invited" isn't enough, one must also be "dressed" in righteousness.

The Ten Virgins (Matthew 25:1-13)

Context

This is one of the final parables in Matthew and comes as part of Jesus' eschatological discourse, dealing with end-times and preparedness for the coming of the Kingdom.

Summary

Ten virgins take their lamps to meet the bridegroom. Five are wise and bring extra oil, while five are foolish and do not. When the bridegroom arrives, only the wise virgins are ready and enter the feast, while the foolish ones are shut out.

Interpretation

The bridegroom represents Christ, and the virgins symbolize those awaiting his return. The parable emphasizes the importance of being spiritually prepared for the unpredictable timing of the Kingdom's full realization.

Theological Implications

This parable underlines the need for vigilant preparedness and wisdom as we await Christ's return. It suggests that spiritual complacency can lead to being excluded from the Kingdom.

Points for Reflection

- The parable prompts us to ask whether we are living in a state of preparedness for Christ's return. Are we "wise" or "foolish" in our spiritual practices?

- It challenges us to consider what "oil" we might need to sustain our spiritual lives over the long haul.

The Talents (Matthew 25:14-30)

Context

Like the Ten Virgins, this parable is part of Jesus' discourse on end-times and speaks to issues of stewardship and responsibility.

Summary

A man going on a journey entrusts his property to his servants according to their abilities. Two of them invest and double their money, while one buries his portion. The master rewards the first two and condemns the last one for his lack of initiative.

Interpretation

The master represents Christ, and the servants symbolize those who have been entrusted with gifts and responsibilities. The parable stresses the importance of active stewardship and warns against spiritual sloth.

Theological Implications

This parable teaches that God expects us to make good use of the gifts and opportunities He provides. It emphasizes the theme of accountability and suggests that we will be judged according to our efforts.

Points for Reflection

- This parable challenges us to assess how we are using our God-given gifts and opportunities. Are we like the diligent servants, or are we more like the slothful ones?

- It prompts us to consider the nature of God's judgment. How does God evaluate our lives, and what does He expect from us?

The Sheep and the Goats (Matthew 25:31-46)

Context

This passage is part of Jesus' eschatological discourse and follows immediately after the Parable of the Talents. While it's sometimes debated whether this is strictly a parable, the narrative is certainly parabolic in nature and speaks about judgment and the end times.

Summary

When the Son of Man comes in glory, he separates people as a shepherd separates sheep from goats. The "sheep" are commended for caring for Jesus by feeding the hungry, welcoming the stranger, clothing the naked, and visiting the sick and imprisoned. The "goats" are condemned for failing to do these things. Both groups are surprised, asking when they saw Jesus hungry, sick, or imprisoned, and Jesus replies that what was done to "the least of these" was done to him.

Interpretation

The "Son of Man" represents Jesus, and the sheep and goats symbolize those who are judged. The passage emphasizes ethical conduct and works of mercy as the criteria for judgment. It argues that how we treat others, particularly the marginalized, reflects our relationship with Jesus himself.

Theological Implications

This narrative confronts us with the inextricable link between faith and action, making the point that genuine faith results in acts of compassion and justice.

Points for Reflection

- The passage challenges us to evaluate our own lives in light of these criteria. Are we living lives of mercy and compassion?

- It also raises theological questions about the nature of judgment and the relationship between faith and works.

New Cloth on an Old Garment & New Wine in Old Wineskins (Matthew 9:16-17)

Context

These sayings come in a context where Jesus is questioned about his practices concerning fasting. They are proverbial in nature and are used to justify why Jesus' new teachings cannot be fit into old religious frameworks.

Summary

Putting new, unshrunk cloth on an old garment will tear the garment. Similarly, putting new wine into old wineskins will burst the skins.

Interpretation

The old garment and old wineskins represent the old religious systems, while the new cloth and new wine symbolize the teachings and practices Jesus brings. The message is that new teachings require a new framework; they cannot be contained within old systems without causing damage.

Theological Implications

These parables touch on the theme of religious renewal and challenge. They question the viability of old religious systems to accommodate the transformative message of Jesus.

Points for Reflection

- These sayings challenge us to consider how open we are to new understandings of faith.

- They also make us question whether our current frameworks—whether they be religious, ethical, or conceptual—are flexible enough to accommodate new truths.

THE LOST SHEEP IN MATTHEW (MATTHEW 18:12-14)

Context

This parable appears in a chapter that deals with the community of disciples and how to handle sin and conflict within it. The emphasis here is somewhat different from Luke's version.

Summary

A man has 100 sheep and loses one. He leaves the 99 to search for the lost one and rejoices when he finds it.

Interpretation

The shepherd represents God or Jesus, and the sheep represent the community of believers. Unlike Luke's version, Matthew's seems to focus more on restoring a wayward member within the faith community.

Theological Implications

This parable speaks of God's deep concern for each individual and the lengths to which God will go to restore someone who has gone astray.

Points for Reflection

- This version of the parable asks us to consider how communities should deal with wayward members. Is restoration and inclusion the aim?

- It also touches on each individual's intrinsic value in God's eyes.

General Themes in Mark's Parables

The Gospel of Mark contains fewer parables than Matthew or Luke, but the parables it does include are powerful and packed with meaning. Here are some general themes found in the parables unique to or prominently featured in Mark:

The Mystery and Paradox of the Kingdom

The Parable of the Seed Growing Secretly (Mark 4:26-29) illustrates the mystery and automatic growth of God's Kingdom. Here, the Kingdom is likened to a seed that grows of its own accord, emphasizing the paradox that while human action is necessary (sowing the seed), the growth itself is out of human control.

The Gradual Unfolding of the Kingdom

In the Parable of the Sower (Mark 4:1-20), we see different responses to the word of God, with the good soil yielding an increasing harvest, illustrating the gradual unfolding of the Kingdom in individual lives and in the world at large.

Small Beginnings, Expansive Outcomes

The Parable of the Mustard Seed (Mark 4:30-32) tells of how the smallest of all seeds becomes the largest of all garden plants, symbolizing the modest beginnings and the eventual, expansive growth of God's Kingdom.

The Newness of Jesus' Message

The parables of the New Cloth on an Old Garment and New Wine in Old Wineskins (Mark 2:21-22) illustrate the incompatibility of the fresh, liberating message of Jesus with the old forms of religion and ritual, pointing to the transformative power of His teachings.

Human Responsibility and Divine Activity

Mark's parables often touch on the interplay between human action and divine intervention. For instance, in the Parable of the Sower, human responsibility is indicated by the different soil types, representing our receptivity to God's word. Meanwhile, the growth of the seed is portrayed as God's own doing in the Parable of the Seed Growing Secretly.

The Call to Discernment

In Mark, the parables serve as teachings and tests that compel the listener to seek understanding. Jesus often uses parables to distinguish between those genuinely seeking God and those not, as evidenced by His explanation for speaking in parables in Mark 4:10-12.

The Urgency of Response

While this is a more implicit theme, the very act of Jesus telling these parables, in a sense, creates an environment of decision. The listener is compelled to respond, to make a choice about how to receive the message.

The Gospel of Mark is the shortest of the four canonical gospels and contains fewer parables than Matthew and Luke. Here's a point-form summary for each parable found in Mark:

The Sower (Mark 4:1-20)

- **Summary**: A sower scatters seed on different types of soil.

- **Key Themes**: Variability in receptiveness to God's word; fruitful and unfruitful responses.

The Seed Growing Secretly (Mark 4:26-29)

- **Summary**: A man scatters seed and it grows without his understanding.

- **Key Themes**: The mystery of the Kingdom of God; growth by divine action.

The Mustard Seed (Mark 4:30-32)

- **Summary**: Tiny mustard seed grows into a large plant.

- **Key Themes**: The Kingdom of God starts small but has an expansive reach.

New Cloth on an Old Garment (Mark 2:21)

- **Summary**: New cloth should not be sewn onto old garments.

- **Key Themes**: Incompatibility of the old and new; transformative power of Jesus' teachings.

New Wine in Old Wineskins (Mark 2:22)

- **Summary**: New wine should be put in new wineskins, not old ones.

- **Key Themes**: The newness of Jesus' teachings; incompatibility with old religious forms.

In summary, although fewer in number, Mark's parables serve as profound teachings on the nature of the Kingdom of God, human responsibility, divine activity, and the radical newness introduced by Jesus. These themes reinforce Mark's overall portrait of Jesus as a mysterious, powerful figure who inaugurates God's Kingdom in surprising ways.

The Sower (Mark 4:3-9, 13-20)

Context

This is one of the few parables in Mark that Jesus also gives an interpretation. It appears early in his ministry, setting the stage for people's different responses to his message.

Summary

A sower scatters seed on various types of ground: the path, rocky ground, thorny ground, and good soil. Only the seed that falls on good soil yields a crop.

Interpretation

The sower represents God or Jesus, and the seed symbolizes the word of God. The different types of soil stand for different kinds of responses to the word. This parable emphasizes the importance of receptivity to the word of God.

Theological Implications

The parable explores the efficacy of the word of God, suggesting that its impact largely depends on the receptiveness and condition of the hearer's heart.

Points for Reflection

- This parable prompts us to assess our own "soil condition." Are we receptive to spiritual truths or let them get choked by life's worries and distractions?

- It also challenges us to consider the quality of our spiritual receptivity and growth. Are we producing fruit?

The Seed Growing Secretly (Mark 4:26-29)

Context

This is unique to Mark's Gospel and comes right after the Parable of the Sower. It speaks about the mysterious growth of the Kingdom of God.

Summary

A man scatters seed on the ground and sleeps. The seed sprouts and grows, though the man does not know how. When the grain is ripe, he harvests it.

Interpretation

The man represents anyone who disseminates God's word or works for the Kingdom. The seed is the word or the Kingdom itself. The focus here is on the mysterious, almost automatic, growth of the Kingdom once the seed is sown.

Theological Implications

This parable focuses on the divine aspect of the Kingdom's growth, emphasizing that ultimately, it is God who gives the increase, independent of human understanding or effort.

Points for Reflection

- The parable reassures those who work for the Kingdom that their efforts are not in vain; God is at work even when we can't see it.

- It also raises the question of trust. Can we trust God to bring about his Kingdom, even when we don't see immediate results?

THE MUSTARD SEED (MARK 4:30-32)

Context

This parable appears in a section focused on the nature and growth of the Kingdom. It serves as a companion piece to the preceding parables in Mark 4.

Summary

The Kingdom of God is like a mustard seed, which is the smallest seed but grows to become the largest of all garden plants, providing shelter for birds.

Interpretation

The mustard seed represents the Kingdom of God, emphasizing its small beginnings and extraordinary growth. The focus is on the surprising and expansive growth of the Kingdom from seemingly insignificant origins.

Theological Implications

The parable speaks to the transformative and expansive nature of God's Kingdom. It emphasizes the potential for enormous impact that lies in small beginnings.

Points for Reflection

- This parable encourages us not to despise small beginnings, either in our personal spiritual journey or in the work of the Kingdom.

- It challenges us to see the potential for Kingdom growth in even the most unlikely or humble of circumstances.

New Cloth on an Old Garment & New Wine in Old Wineskins (Mark 2:21-22)

Context and Summary

These appear early in Mark's Gospel in a section that portrays Jesus as challenging traditional religious practices, specifically fasting. Their content is similar to the versions in Matthew and Luke.

Interpretation and Theological Implications

As in Matthew, the old garment and wineskins represent existing religious practices, while the new cloth and wine symbolize Jesus' teachings. The new cannot be made to fit into the old without causing problems, highlighting the revolutionary nature of Jesus' message.

Points for Reflection

- These parables raise questions about our own religious or spiritual frameworks. Are they flexible enough to accommodate fresh understandings of faith?

- They also prompt us to consider whether we're trying to fit the new teachings of Jesus into old, potentially incompatible systems or practices.

General Themes in Luke's Parables

Let's explore the general themes in the parables in the Gospel of Luke. These themes offer an encompassing view of the key messages that Luke aims to convey through the teachings of Jesus:

God's Boundless Mercy and Grace

Many of Luke's parables, such as The Good Samaritan, The Prodigal Son, and The Lost Sheep, emphasize the theme of God's compassion and limitless grace extended toward humanity. They underscore the idea that God's love transcends traditional boundaries, be they social, religious, or moral.

Joy and Celebration in Repentance

Parables like The Lost Sheep, The Lost Coin, and The Prodigal Son feature a strong emphasis on the joy and celebration that accompany repentance. They reflect God's own joy when a sinner turns back to Him, contrasting it with the human tendency to judge or exclude.

The Challenge to Religious Self-Righteousness

Several parables, such as The Pharisee and the Tax Collector and The Good Samaritan, challenge the religious self-righteousness of their audience. They turn expected social and religious hierarchies upside down, presenting religious leaders in a poor light while elevating societal outcasts.

Social Justice and Compassion

Luke's parables often have a social or ethical dimension, emphasizing acts of compassion and justice. The Good Samaritan and The Rich Man and Lazarus serve as ethical injunctions to care for the needy and marginalized, signaling a form of practical theology deeply concerned with social justice.

The Necessity and Effectiveness of Prayer

The Friend at Midnight and The Unjust Judge deal directly with the theme of prayer, emphasizing its importance and efficacy. These parables encourage a persistent, shameless, and expectant attitude in prayer.

Judgment and the Kingdom of God

Parables like The Rich Fool and The Rich Man and Lazarus offer cautionary tales about the eternal consequences of one's choices on earth, with a focus on materialism and neglect of the poor. They remind the audience of the impending divine judgment and the ethical demands of life in the Kingdom of God.

Divine Reversal

The Great Banquet and other parables speak to the theme of divine reversal, where the first shall be last and the last shall be first in the Kingdom of God. These parables often highlight God's predilection for the poor, the outcast, and the sinner over the self-righteous or the complacent.

Stewardship and Accountability

Parables like The Dishonest Manager and The Ten Minas touch upon the theme of stewardship, emphasizing the responsible management of resources—be they material, social, or spiritual—in preparation for the coming Kingdom.

Wisdom in Worldly and Spiritual Matters

Several of Luke's parables, like The Dishonest Manager, balance worldly wisdom with spiritual priorities, indicating that one can be shrewd in worldly dealings while maintaining integrity and focus on the Kingdom of God.

Through these various themes, Luke crafts a multifaceted portrayal of the teachings of Jesus, which are aimed at both the individual's inner spiritual life and the broader social and ethical obligations to the community. Each theme contributes to Luke's overarching narrative and theological points, rounding out a diverse and comprehensive understanding of the Gospel message.

Here's a comprehensive summary of the parables discussed from the Gospel of Luke, each touching upon various facets of spiritual and ethical life:

The Sower (Luke 8:4-15)

- **Summary**: Seeds sown on different types of ground yield varying results.

- **Key Themes**: Receptivity to God's word; different outcomes based on soil conditions.

The Lamp Under a Jar (Luke 8:16-18)

- **Summary**: A lamp is not hidden but placed to give light to all.

- **Key Themes**: The revealing nature of truth; responsibility to share the message.

The Wise and Foolish Builders (Luke 6:46-49)

- **Summary**: Two builders, wise and foolish, build houses on different foundations.

- **Key Themes**: Importance of a strong foundation in faith; wisdom vs. foolishness.

The Mustard Seed (Luke 13:18-19)

- **Summary**: Small mustard seed grows into large tree.

- **Key Themes**: The expansive growth of the Kingdom of God; humble beginnings.

The Leaven (Luke 13:20-21)

- **Summary**: Yeast spreads through dough.

- **Key Themes**: Pervasive influence of the Kingdom; small beginnings to significant results.

The Good Samaritan (Luke 10:25-37)

- **Summary**: Samaritan helps injured man, unlike priest and Levite.

- **Key Themes**: Redefining neighborliness; critique of religious hypocrisy.

The Friend at Midnight (Luke 11:5-13)

- **Summary**: Persistent friend receives what he asks for.

- **Key Themes**: Importance of persistence in prayer; God's willingness to give.

The Rich Fool (Luke 12:13-21)

- **Summary**: Rich man hoards wealth, dies before he can enjoy it.

- **Key Themes**: Folly of greed; transient nature of material wealth.

The Barren Fig Tree (Luke 13:6-9)

- **Summary**: Fruitless fig tree given another chance to produce fruit.

- **Key Themes**: Divine patience and judgment; opportunity for repentance.

The Great Banquet (Luke 14:15-24)

- **Summary**: Invited guests make excuses; the poor and marginalized are invited.

- **Key Themes**: The inclusive nature of God's Kingdom; rejection by the initially invited.

The Lost Sheep (Luke 15:1-7)

- **Summary**: Shepherd leaves 99 sheep to find one lost sheep.

- **Key Themes**: God's care for the lost; joy over repentance.

The Lost Coin (Luke 15:8-10)

- **Summary**: Woman searches for a lost coin and rejoices upon finding it.

- **Key Themes**: God's diligent search for the lost; joy in heaven over one sinner's repentance.

The Prodigal Son (Luke 15:11-32)

- **Summary**: Younger son wastes inheritance but is welcomed back by his father.

- **Key Themes**: God's unconditional love; repentance and forgiveness.

The Dishonest Manager (Luke 16:1-13)

- **Summary**: Unjust steward reduces debts to gain favor.

- **Key Themes**: Use of worldly wealth for eternal benefits; faithfulness in small things.

The Rich Man and Lazarus (Luke 16:19-31)

- **Summary**: Rich man and poor Lazarus die; roles are reversed in the afterlife.

- **Key Themes**: Social justice; eternal consequences of earthly choices.

The Unjust Judge (Luke 18:1-8)

- **Summary**: Persistent widow receives justice from an uncaring judge.

- **Key Themes**: Persistence in prayer; God's justice.

The Pharisee and the Tax Collector (Luke 18:9-14)

- **Summary**: Pharisee prays boastfully; tax collector humbly asks for mercy.

- **Key Themes**: Humility vs. self-righteousness; justification through humility.

The Ten Minas (Luke 19:11-27)

- **Summary**: Servants are given minas to invest; various returns lead to various rewards.

- **Key Themes**: Stewardship; faithfulness in service.

New Cloth on an Old Garment & New Wine in Old Wineskins (Luke 5:36-39)

- **Summary**: New cloth and new wine are incompatible with old garments and old wineskins.

- **Key Themes**: Incompatibility of old and new religious forms; Jesus' new teachings.

Through these parables, the Gospel of Luke offers a vastness of teachings on the Kingdom of God, social ethics, prayer, repentance, and the dangers of materialism and self-righteousness. They serve as potent tools for self-examination and offer insight into the character and priorities of God.

THE SOWER (LUKE 8:5-15)

Context

This parable appears in the context of Jesus' early public ministry, where He is teaching large crowds. It sets the stage for different kinds of responses to His message.

Summary

A sower scatters seeds on various types of ground: the path, rocky soil, thorny ground, and good soil. Each type of soil produces a different result, with only the seed in good soil yielding a good crop.

Interpretation

Like in Matthew and Mark, the seed symbolizes the word of God, and the types of ground represent the various responses to it. Luke's version emphasizes "hearing the word, retaining it, and by persevering produce a crop."

Theological Implications

The parable presents a kind of spiritual taxonomy, categorizing hearers into different types based on their responsiveness to the word of God.

Points for Reflection

- What type of soil are you? Are you open to God's word, or are there obstacles that hinder it from taking root in your life?

- The parable also prompts self-examination: are you producing spiritual "fruit"?

The Lamp Under a Jar (Luke 8:16-18)

Context

This parable follows immediately after the Parable of the Sower, reinforcing its themes and expanding on the idea of revelation and concealment.

Summary

A lamp is not lit to be put under a jar but to be placed on a stand so its light may benefit everyone in the house.

Interpretation

The lamp likely symbolizes the message of the Kingdom or the truth of God's word. Hiding it is counterproductive to its nature and purpose.

Theological Implications

The parable speaks to the public proclamation of the gospel and the role of believers in disseminating God's word.

Points for Reflection

- Are you hiding your "light," or are you putting it in a place where it can illuminate others?

- It also serves as a warning to be cautious about what we "hear" or how we respond to God's word.

The Wise and the Foolish Builders (Luke 6:46-49)

Context

This parable is the conclusion to the "Sermon on the Plain" in Luke, equivalent to the "Sermon on the Mount" in Matthew.

Summary

Two builders build houses, one on a rock and another on sand. When a storm comes, only the house built on the rock stands firm.

Interpretation

The house symbolizes one's life, and the foundation is one's response to Jesus' teachings. The wise builder is one who not only hears but acts on them.

Theological Implications

The parable stresses the importance of not just hearing but living out God's word as the basis for a stable spiritual life.

Points for Reflection

- Are you building your life on the firm foundation of Jesus' teachings?

- It encourages us to self-examine our actions against our professed beliefs.

THE MUSTARD SEED (LUKE 13:18-19)

Context

This parable is found in a section where Jesus is teaching about the Kingdom of God. It serves as a companion to other parables on the Kingdom's growth and nature.

Summary

The Kingdom of God is compared to a mustard seed, which is very small but grows into a large tree, providing shelter to the birds.

Interpretation

The mustard seed symbolizes the Kingdom of God, emphasizing its initially small size and surprising growth into something substantial and influential.

Theological Implications

This parable emphasizes the transformative and expansive power of God's Kingdom, from humble beginnings to significant impact.

Points for Reflection

- The parable challenges us to look for the Kingdom of God in small or overlooked places.

- It reminds us of the potential for extraordinary growth in seemingly ordinary things when they are infused with the Kingdom's power.

The Leaven (Luke 13:20-21)

Context

The Leaven follows the Mustard Seed parable and continues to describe the Kingdom of God.

Summary

The Kingdom is likened to leaven, which a woman takes and hides in three measures of flour until the whole thing is leavened.

Interpretation

The leaven symbolizes the pervasive and transformative nature of the Kingdom of God.

Theological Implications

The Kingdom of God is not just growing in size (as in the Mustard Seed parable) but also in influence, permeating and transforming society from within.

Points for Reflection

- How are we allowing the Kingdom to "leaven" our lives, trans-forming us from within?

- The parable also prompts us to think about how the Kingdom of God is meant to influence society at large.

The Good Samaritan (Luke 10:30-37)

Context

This iconic parable is given in response to a lawyer's question about who his neighbor is, after Jesus sums up the law as love for God and neighbor.

Summary

In the parable, a man is traveling from Jerusalem to Jericho, a notoriously dangerous road known for its steep cliffs and hiding places for robbers. Sure enough, the man falls victim to thieves, who beat him up, strip him of his clothes, and leave him half-dead by the roadside.

First, a priest comes along the same path. When he sees the man, he crosses over to the other side of the road and continues on his way, making no effort to help. Next, a Levite appears. He also notices the man but chooses to pass by on the other side, ignoring the injured traveler. These were people who, according to the religious standards of the time, should have been the epitome of moral and ethical behavior. Yet, both fail to act.

Finally, a Samaritan appears on the scene. Samaritans were often despised by Jews; they were considered religious and social outcasts. However, this Samaritan is moved with compassion upon seeing the injured man. He goes over to him, cleans his wounds with oil and wine, and bandages them. Then, he places the man on his own animal and takes him to an inn, where he continues to take care of him. The next day, the Samaritan gives the innkeeper two denarii (a form of currency), instructs him to look after the wounded man, and promises to pay any additional costs upon his return.

Jesus concludes the parable by asking the lawyer who had initially raised the question about neighbors, "Which of these three, do you think, proved to be a neighbor to the man who fell among the robbers?" The lawyer replies, "The one who showed him mercy." Jesus then instructs him to "Go and do likewise."

Interpretation

The parable redefines the concept of "neighbor" and shatters pre-existing cultural and religious barriers.

Theological Implications

It calls for a radical, selfless love that transcends social, ethnic, or religious boundaries.

Points for Reflection

- It challenges us to rethink who our "neighbors" are.

- Are we willing to show compassion even when it's inconvenient or costly?

The Friend at Midnight (Luke 11:5-8)

Context

This parable comes right after the disciples ask Jesus to teach them how to pray, and Jesus provides what is commonly known as the Lord's Prayer. The parable is aimed at illustrating the importance of persistent prayer.

Summary

At midnight, a man goes to his friend's house to ask for three loaves of bread. The friend is initially reluctant, pointing out that his family is already in bed. However, because of the man's persistence, he eventually gets up and gives him the bread.

Interpretation

The parable is often understood as an encouragement for persistent prayer. It's not that God is reluctant to give good gifts to those who ask, but persistence in prayer is commended and effective.

Theological Implications

The story illustrates how prayer is not just a one-off request but an ongoing relationship that involves persistence. God's response is not because of the annoyance but because of the relationship and the earnestness involved in asking.

Points for Reflection

- How persistent are you in your prayer life? Are there things you've given up praying for?

- It reminds us that God values our sincere and repeated petitions, which can deepen our relationship with Him.

The Rich Fool (Luke 12:16-21)

Context

This parable is presented in the context of a warning against all kinds of greed and comes as a response to a man in the crowd who asks Jesus to tell his brother to divide the family inheritance with him.

Summary

A rich man's fields produce a bumper crop, and he decides to tear down his existing barns to build bigger ones to store all his grain and goods. He plans to take it easy, eat, drink, and be merry. But God says to him, "You fool! This very night your life will be demanded from you. Then who will get what you have prepared for yourself?"

Interpretation

The parable warns against the foolishness of placing one's ultimate trust in material wealth, especially at the neglect of one's spiritual well-being.

Theological Implications

It speaks to the transient nature of life and the folly of storing up earthly treasures at the expense of gaining a rich relationship with God.

Points for Reflection

- The parable prompts us to consider where our real treasure lies. Are we investing more in the material world than in our spiritual life?

- It also serves as a stark reminder of the unpredictability and fragility of life.

THE BARREN FIG TREE (LUKE 13:6-9)

Context

This parable appears in a chapter where Jesus is discussing the themes of repentance and judgment. It comes right after Jesus talks about two tragic incidents, urging his listeners to repent.

Summary

A man has a fig tree planted in his vineyard, but it does not produce fruit for three years. He considers cutting it down, but the vineyard keeper suggests giving it one more year with special care to see if it will bear fruit.

Interpretation

The barren fig tree is often understood as symbolizing the people of Israel or humanity in general. The lack of fruit represents the absence of righteousness or good deeds, and the owner's patience represents God's mercy.

Theological Implications

The parable emphasizes the patience and long-suffering of God but also the urgency and necessity of repentance. There's a finite window of opportunity to produce "fruit."

Points for Reflection

- The parable serves as a cautionary tale to not waste our opportunities for spiritual growth and moral integrity.

- It calls us to take time and effort to nurture our spiritual lives so that they bear fruit.

The Great Banquet (Luke 14:15-24)

Context

Jesus tells this parable during a dinner at a Pharisee's house. It comes right after He advises the host to invite the poor and needy rather than friends and relatives who can repay him.

Summary

A man hosts a great banquet and invites many guests. When the time comes, the guests make various excuses not to attend. The host then invites the poor, crippled, blind, and lame. Even after that, there is still room, so the host commands his servant to go out to the roads and compel people to come in to fill his house.

Interpretation

The great banquet symbolizes God's Kingdom, and the initial invitees who decline the invitation are those who reject God's offer, usually for mundane reasons. The subsequent invitees represent those who would typically be excluded but are now welcomed.

Theological Implications

This parable shows God's generosity and inclusivity but also human short-sightedness and priorities that can make us miss the most significant invitation of our lives.

Points for Reflection

- Are we prioritizing God's invitation to partake in His Kingdom, or are we too engrossed in worldly matters?

- It also speaks to the inclusivity of the Kingdom of God, inviting all, irrespective of social standing.

The Lost Sheep (Luke 15:3-7)

Context

This parable is part of a trio of "lost and found" parables in Luke 15, which also includes the Lost Coin and the Prodigal Son. Jesus tells these parables in response to the Pharisees and scribes who criticize Him for welcoming and eating with "sinners."

Summary

A shepherd has 100 sheep, and one of them goes missing. He leaves the 99 in the wilderness to search for the lost one. When he finds it, he rejoices and carries it home, calling his friends and neighbors to celebrate.

Interpretation

The lost sheep represents a sinner who has strayed from the path of righteousness. The shepherd symbolizes God, who actively seeks out the lost to bring them back to the fold.

Theological Implications

The parable underscores God's immense love for each individual and His desire for their return to righteousness. It also critiques the self-righteous attitude of those who look down on the "lost."

Points for Reflection

- Are we willing to leave our comfort zones to seek the lost and bring them back to the fold?

- It challenges our attitudes towards those who are considered "outcasts" or "sinners."

The Lost Coin (Luke 15:8-10)

Context

The Lost Coin follows the Lost Sheep in the same chapter and addresses the same audience for the same reason: to defend Jesus' outreach to sinners.

Summary

A woman has ten silver coins and loses one. She lights a lamp, sweeps her house, and searches diligently until she finds it. When she does, she calls her friends and neighbors to celebrate.

Interpretation

Similarly to the Lost Sheep, the lost coin represents a sinner, and the woman represents God or Jesus, who actively seeks and rejoices in the repentance of the lost.

Theological Implications

This parable also emphasizes the value God places on each individual soul and His relentless pursuit to save even one.

Points for Reflection

- It invites us to take part in the joy that heaven experiences when one sinner repents.

- How diligent are we in our efforts to find what's lost in our lives, be it faith, purpose, or relationships?

The Prodigal Son (Luke 15:11-32)

Context

This is the third parable in Luke 15, coming right after the Lost Sheep and the Lost Coin. The context is the same: Jesus is responding to criticism from the religious leaders about His association with sinners.

Summary

A younger son asks his father for his share of the inheritance and goes to spend it all in a far-off country on loose living. When a famine arises, he finds himself in dire straits and decides to return home and ask for his father's forgiveness. The father sees him from a distance, runs to him, and embraces him, ordering a feast in his honor. The older son, however, is resentful of this treatment and confronts the father, who reassures him, saying that all he has is his but that they should still celebrate the lost son's return.

Interpretation

The prodigal son represents the repentant sinner, and the father represents God's unconditional love and forgiveness. The older brother symbolizes the self-righteous who resent God's grace extended to repentant sinners.

Theological Implications

The parable provides profound insights into the nature of repentance, forgiveness, and God's overwhelming grace and love. It also critiques self-righteousness and the failure to rejoice at the repentance of sinners.

Points for Reflection

- The parable prompts us to reflect on the nature of God's love and how we respond to it, both as recipients and observers.

- It also challenges our attitudes toward grace and mercy, especially when extended to those we don't think deserve it.

The Dishonest Manager (Luke 16:1-13)

Context

This parable comes in a chapter following the "lost and found" series. The audience appears to be the disciples, but the Pharisees also listen in and are rebuked later in the chapter.

Summary

A rich man's manager is accused of wasting his possessions. When he finds out he's going to be fired, the manager shrewdly reduces the debts owed to his master by various debtors, hoping they'll take him in after losing his job. The master commends him for his shrewdness, though not for his dishonesty. Jesus then talks about the importance of being faithful in small things to be trusted with greater things, as well as the impossibility of serving God and money.

Interpretation

This is one of the more puzzling parables. While the dishonest manager is not praised for his dishonesty, he is commended for his shrewdness. The lesson seems to be that if even dishonest people are clever in dealing with their worldly affairs, how much more should the righteous be in heavenly matters.

Theological Implications

The parable touches on themes of stewardship, resourcefulness, and the tension between worldly wealth and spiritual riches.

Points for Reflection

- How wisely are we using our resources for eternal benefit?

- It urges us to think about our ultimate loyalties: are we serving God or wealth?

The Rich Man and Lazarus (Luke 16:19-31)

Context

This parable follows the Dishonest Manager and is primarily directed at the Pharisees, who were described as lovers of money. It serves to confront their misguided values.

Summary

A rich man lives in luxury, while a poor man named Lazarus sits at his gate, covered in sores and longing for crumbs from the rich man's table. Both men die; angels carry Lazarus to Abraham's side, and the rich man ends up in Hades. In torment, the rich man sees Lazarus at peace with Abraham and asks for relief, but it's too late. He then asks Abraham to send Lazarus to warn his brothers, but Abraham says they have the Law and the Prophets to guide them. The rich man insists that someone from the dead will persuade them, but Abraham retorts that if they don't listen to Scripture, they won't be convinced even if someone rises from the dead.

Interpretation

The parable contrasts the eternal destinies that await the righteous and the wicked. It is a cautionary tale about the perils of wealth when it breeds indifference and neglect toward the suffering.

Theological Implications

The parable addresses the relationship between earthly conduct and eternal consequences. It emphasizes the importance of the Scriptures as a guide to righteous living.

Points for Reflection

- The story prompts us to consider how we use our resources and whether we are sensitive to the suffering around us.

- It also serves as a wake-up call to take spiritual truths and Scriptures seriously.

THE UNJUST JUDGE (LUKE 18:1-8)

Context

This parable is introduced explicitly as a lesson on the importance of persistent prayer and not losing heart.

Summary

A widow repeatedly goes to an unjust judge to grant her justice against her adversary. Initially, the judge is reluctant but eventually gives in because he is annoyed by her persistence.

Interpretation

The widow represents the believer, and the unjust judge symbolizes God, though the comparison is more of a contrast. If even an unjust judge will act due to persistence, how much more will a loving God respond to persistent prayer?

Theological Implications

The parable encourages persistent prayer and assures us of God's ultimate justice and responsiveness.

Points for Reflection

- It invites us to examine our own prayer life: Are we persistent in bringing our concerns to God?

- It also reassures that justice will be done, even when earthly systems fail.

THE PHARISEE AND THE TAX COLLECTOR (LUKE 18:9-14)

Context

The parable is directed towards "some who were confident of their own righteousness and looked down on everyone else," serving as a corrective to self-righteous attitudes and promoting humility.

Summary

Two men go to the temple to pray. One is a Pharisee who thanks God that he is not like other people—robbers, evildoers, adulterers—or even like the tax collector. He mentions that he fasts twice a week and gives a tenth of all he gets. The tax collector, however, stands far off and won't even look up to heaven. He simply prays, "God, have mercy on me, a sinner." Jesus says the tax collector went home justified, not the Pharisee.

Interpretation

The Pharisee symbolizes self-righteousness and complacency, while the tax collector represents humility and a keen awareness of one's sinfulness.

Theological Implications

The parable fundamentally critiques the self-righteous and lifts up the contrite. It emphasizes the role of grace in justification, as opposed to self-righteous deeds.

Points for Reflection

- It forces us to examine our attitudes in prayer and our perception of others.

- The parable challenges us to approach God humbly, recognizing our need for mercy.

THE TEN MINAS (LUKE 19:11-27)

Context

This parable is told because Jesus was nearing Jerusalem, and the people thought the kingdom of God was going to appear at once. It aims to correct misunderstandings about the immediacy of the kingdom's establishment.

Summary

A man of noble birth goes to a distant country to be appointed king and then returns. He gives ten minas (a very large sum of a unit of currency) to ten of his servants and tells them to "put this money to work" until he returns. Upon his return, the first servant has earned ten more minas and is rewarded. The second earns five more and is also rewarded. A third servant, however, has hidden the mina and is rebuked. The mina is taken from him and given to the one who has ten.

Interpretation

The nobleman represents Jesus, and the servants represent His followers. The parable focuses on responsible stewardship during the "already but not yet" period of the kingdom of God.

Theological Implications

The parable addresses the idea of the Kingdom of God being both present and future. It also talks about the necessity of faithful service in the interim.

Points for Reflection

- How are we using the resources—time, talents, treasure—that God has given us?

- Are we anticipating the return of Christ with diligent service?

New Cloth on an Old Garment & New Wine in Old Wineskins (Luke 5:36-39)

Context

Jesus tells these parables in response to questions about why His disciples do not fast like John's disciples and the Pharisees.

Summary

In the first, new cloth should not be sewn onto an old garment, or else the new patch will shrink and tear the old cloth. In the second, new wine must be poured into new wineskins, or else the skins will burst.

Interpretation

Both parables deal with the incompatibility of the new covenant in Christ with the old covenant based on the Law.

Theological Implications

They point to the transformational power of Christ's teachings and the inadequacy of old religious systems to contain this new reality.

Points for Reflection

- Are we open to the newness of Christ's message, or are we stuck in old paradigms?

- These parables challenge us to be flexible in our understanding of God's unfolding plan.

GENERAL THEMES IN JOHN'S PARABLES

While the Gospel of John doesn't contain parables in the traditional sense, it does present allegorical teachings that serve to elucidate spiritual truths, much like parables do in the Synoptic Gospels (Matthew, Mark, Luke). These extended metaphors or allegories also express overarching themes, which are deeply embedded within the larger theological framework of John's Gospel. Here are some general themes found in the allegorical teachings of John:

Divine Relationship and Intimacy

- Seen in both "The Good Shepherd" and "The Vine and the Branches," these allegories stress the intimate relationship between Jesus and His followers.

- The idea of "abiding" in Christ (as branches in the vine) emphasizes an ongoing, deeply connected relationship with Him.

Leadership and Authority of Christ

- In "The Good Shepherd," Jesus is presented as the ultimate leader who knows His flock intimately and sacrifices Himself for their well-being.

- This underscores His unique authority and contrasts Him with false leaders or "thieves and robbers" who do not have the best interests of the flock at heart.

Sacrifice and Self-Giving Love

- Both allegories touch on the notion of sacrificial love, but it is most explicit in "The Good Shepherd," where Jesus states that He lays down His life for His sheep.

- This theme aligns closely with the Johannine emphasis on Jesus' sacrificial death as an act of love.

Spiritual Fruitfulness

- The allegory of "The Vine and the Branches" focuses on the idea of bearing spiritual fruit.

- This concept is tied to the idea of abiding in Jesus. Those who remain connected to Him will naturally produce good fruit, which can be understood as ethical living, effective ministry, and deepening faith.

Divine Selection and Pruning

- In "The Vine and the Branches," the act of pruning by the "gardener" (interpreted as God the Father) symbolizes divine discipline and refinement.

- This serves as a way to optimize the spiritual growth and fruitfulness of believers.

Eschatological Implications

- While not as explicit as in some Synoptic parables, these allegories have a future orientation, especially seen in the protective role of the Good Shepherd, who provides eternal life to His sheep.

- In "The Vine and the Branches," the ultimate goal is to bear lasting fruit, hinting at eternal rewards or consequences.

These general themes are inextricable from the broader theological messages of the Gospel of John, which deepen our understanding of the nature and mission of Jesus Christ and the responsibilities and privileges of His followers.

John employs extended metaphors or allegories, such as "The Good Shepherd" and "The Vine and the Branches," which serve a similar purpose in illustrating spiritual truths. Here are brief summaries:

The Good Shepherd (John 10:1-18)

- **Summary**: Jesus describes Himself as the good shepherd who lays down His life for the sheep.

- **Key Themes**: Leadership, sacrifice, and intimate knowledge between Jesus and His followers.

The Vine and the Branches (John 15:1-17)

- **Summary**: Jesus is the true vine and His followers are the branches, which must remain in Him to bear fruit.

- **Key Themes**: Abiding in Christ, spiritual fruitfulness, and divine pruning for growth.

These allegorical teachings in John are rich and layered, often over-lapping with themes found in the Synoptic parables but presented in a manner more integrated with the narrative.

The Good Shepherd (John 10:1-18)

Context

This allegory is presented in John 10, following the story of the healing of the man born blind in John 9. Jesus is addressing a mixed audience of His followers and religious leaders, drawing a contrast between His leadership and that of the Pharisees.

Summary

Jesus identifies Himself as the "Good Shepherd" who enters through the gate, contrasting Himself with "thieves and robbers" who climb in some other way. He describes how the sheep hear His voice, and He calls them by name, leading them out to pasture.

The Good Shepherd is willing to lay down His life for the sheep, in contrast to a "hired hand" who abandons them when danger comes.

Interpretation

Jesus is claiming to be the true leader who cares for His people deeply, to the point of sacrificing His own life. The sheep represent those who recognize and follow Jesus, implying an intimate, personal relationship between the shepherd and his flock.

Theological Implications

The image of Jesus as the Good Shepherd has deep Old Testament roots (Psalms 23, Ezekiel 34).

It emphasizes His divine authority, sacrificial love, and the protective, guiding relationship He has with His followers.

Points of Reflection

- How do you respond to the voice of the "Good Shepherd" in your life?

- What does it mean to you that Jesus, as the Good Shepherd, was willing to lay down His life for you?

The Vine and the Branches (John 15:1-17)

Context

This allegory occurs within the context of the "Farewell Discourse," a series of teachings Jesus gave to His disciples during the Last Supper. It follows discussions about love and obedience, preparing the disciples for His impending crucifixion.

Summary

Jesus describes Himself as the "true vine" and His Father as the "gardener" who prunes or cuts off branches. The disciples are the branches expected to bear fruit; they can only do so by remaining attached to the vine, Jesus.

Interpretation

The vine serves as a metaphor for spiritual and communal life centered on Jesus. The act of pruning implies spiritual discipline and purification, designed to increase fruitfulness.

Theological Implications

The allegory underscores the necessity of remaining in a close, dependent relationship with Jesus for spiritual vitality and effectiveness.

It introduces the theme of mutual indwelling ("abide in me, and I in you"), a distinctive Johannine idea.

Points of Reflection

- How are you abiding in Christ, and how is that reflected in your life?

- What might the "pruning" in your spiritual journey look like?

WRAP UP

The parables and allegories in the four Gospels offer profound insights into the nature of God, the kingdom of heaven, and what it means to be a follower of Jesus Christ. Each Gospel writer, through their unique set of parables or allegorical teachings, focuses on specific theological and ethical themes relevant to their audience.

- In **Matthew**, the parables often revolve around the kingdom of heaven and how to enter it. Themes of judgment and reward, societal roles, and divine justice are prevalent.

- **Mark's** shorter list of parables tends to concentrate on the mystery of the Kingdom of God, its unexpected and even paradoxical growth, and the importance of responsive hearing.

- **Luke** focuses on social ethics, compassion, and the expansive grace of God. His parables often feature unexpected heroes and provide a voice to the marginalized.

- **John**, while not employing parables in the traditional sense, uses allegory to delve into themes of divine relationship, leadership, sacrifice, and spiritual fruitfulness.

In all these teachings, we find an invitation to understand God, His kingdom, and His values in ways that defy conventional wisdom. They challenge us to reconsider our attitudes, judgments, and priorities. They call us to a deeper, transformational faith, not merely a ritualistic or sur-face-level religion.

Points for Reflection:

1. **Personal Relevance**: Which parable or allegory resonates most deeply with you at this moment in your spiritual journey? Why?

2. **Kingdom Perspective**: How have these parables challenged or expanded your understanding of the Kingdom of God?

3. **Ethical Implications**: In what ways do these teachings compel you to change your behavior or attitude towards others?

4. **Divine Relationship**: How do the parables and allegories deepen your understanding of your relationship with God?

5. **Theological Curiosity**: Is there a particular theme or concept that you are drawn to explore further?

As you ponder these questions, may you be led into a deeper under-standing and appreciation of these timeless spiritual teachings. Whether you find yourself identifying with a lost sheep, a prodigal son, a shrewd manager, or a branch on a vine, the divine wisdom encapsulated in these narratives offers a pathway for spiritual growth and transformation.

About the Author

Steven Smith has been giving lessons about the Gospels since 2005. The author is an educator and lifelong student, having studied at universities in Canada and the UK. His interest in the Gospels is focused on Jesus's messages of Peace and Love. Steven's inspiration to become an educator comes from his wife, who is a university professor. They have two children, a Jack Russell Terrier, and two rescued cats.

www.ingramcontent.com/pod-product-compliance
Lightning Source LLC
Chambersburg PA
CBHW071202120626
46546CB00006B/2376